ANGEL OF THE HEART

Compiled by

Paula Cruttenden Haines

and Lesley Harris

Published by
Paula Cruttenden Haines
24 Rockliffe Avenue
Bath BA2 6QP

Printed by
Meon Valley Printers
Bishops Waltham

Dedication

In memory of my daughter, Eleanor, and all other children whose untimely deaths shatter the hearts of those who love them.

ISBN 0 9519350 0 3

CONTENTS **PAGE**

Foreword

If it were not for the death of my small daughter Eleanor on 10 September 1989, the idea for this book would never have been born. Eleanor was born prematurely on the 6th September - I was just 25 weeks pregnant. It seems miraculous that she lived at all now, but at that time my desire for her to survive was so strong that I never doubted her strength. She did fight bravely, and during her short life she was seen by our dear friends, Lesley, Jackie and Angelo and by Terry's parents. After many close shaves where we were warned we may lose her she seemed to stabilise, but we were lent false hope she died shortly before her fifth day. Her lungs were just too underdeveloped. The love that we felt for her was overwhelming and her death was shattering. During the early days after her death my husband Terry and I received many cards and letters from friends and colleagues who were as shocked as us at her early arrival and the injustice of her short life. The words people said and wrote to me were so important - they were a life line. They comforted me. Kind words made me cry, and it was so important that I allowed my grief out, even words that made me angry were better than the silence of those who did not know what to say.

Lesley sent me a beautiful poem by Henry Wadsworth Longfellow called 'The Reaper and the Flowers'. It was the saddest thing I'd ever read, and it had been written by someone who had also lost children. It gave me enormous comfort during the days and months of my grieving, even now it still brings a big lump to my throat. Later I realised how very little poetry on the subject there was when a year later I was putting together a programme for a Babies Remembrance Service at the Chapel of the Bath Royal United Hospital. It was impossible to find more than a few modern poems that would be suitable on the subject. It seems the subject is very much taboo in our society, where we are encouraged to hide away our feelings rather than express them. Yet for many knowing how others felt when they also lost a child is such an important source of comfort.

Lesley suggested that we should remedy the situation by putting together an anthology of poems on the death of children so that other people could at least find something on the subject in the future - and so our project began. We aimed to collect as wide a range of material as we could to cover the whole range of child deaths, be they from miscarriage, stillbirth, in infancy and childhood right through to adulthood and to reflect the variety of people affected by a child's death, the parents, the grandparents, brothers, sisters and friends.

Our request first appeared in Woman & Home in November 1990 and later in the Daily Mirror, the newsletters for The Miscarriage Association and The Compassionate Friends and in the poetry magazines Envoi, Acumen and Outposts.

The response was overwhelming, so many wrote to encourage the project and we received nearly 400 poems, some from as far afield as America and Australia. The letters and their poems touched us deeply and we were heartened by the tremendous support people felt for our project. It was this that kept us going when the task seemed insurmountable. It was a difficult choice to select the final poems for inclusion and our thanks goes out to all those that wrote to us. Our special thanks goes to those whose poems are included for whom we can give no reward but whom we hope will feel a special pride in appearing here.

The profits from the sale of this book will go to CRUSE, The Miscarriage Association, The Compassionate Friends and SANDS (Stillbirth and Neonatal Death Society) and will be used to provide help and support to the bereaved. Most importantly we hope that amongst the many poems included you the reader will find some words of comfort to see you through and we hope this encourages you to write your own dedication in memory of the child you mourn.

Paula Cruttenden Haines

I suppose one truism universally recognised, is that you never experience true empathy until you are extremely close to someone. The unthinkable occurs; their beloved child dies, and suddenly and irrevocably, you share their pain and sorrow. That is what happened to me when Eleanor died. Although in the past I have felt sad and sympathetic when friends had miscarriages and when family members spoke of babies and children dying I still felt distanced from it. I never for one moment imagined the complete horror, trauma and desolation that losing a child brings to the parents and all the family and friends that love them. Being the mother of a two year old girl, Eleanor's death was the nightmare scenario that lurks in the back of the mind of every parent.

As a close friend, I found it natural to be able to express my sorrow and to grieve with Paula, and for her and her husband. But there were times, at the funeral for instance, when I was at a loss as to what to say. Poetry for me, seemed a solution to that lapse in communication. The poem that I sent to Paula said everything that I wanted to say, but could not adequately articulate. It was a great comfort to myself at a time when I thought the world was completely black.

Later, on reading the large numbers of poems that we received, it was evident that poetry meant a great deal to many people. Many had one particular poem which had helped them through the most dreadful period of their lives, one perhaps that they had treasured for years and years.

After a lot of thought, looking at poems that were widely known and those that were perhaps being shared for the first time with us, we decided that the content of the new material was so strong and unique that we would concentrate on those.

We soon had a large selection of work that was representative of a group of people who had suffered the agony of losing a child and who had written about it from many different angles. Bereavement councillors advise that some of the usual stages passed through after someone dies are denial, anger, guilt and sorrow. All these emotions are to be found in the book and more.

It has been a great privilege for me to have been a part of this project. I have been left with a renewed faith in the essential goodness of human nature; that people can lose the very dearest person in their lives, but are still able to reach out and share their painful and private experience to benefit others.

Lesley Harris

Farewell, sweet child
Thou shalt ever be
A star to guide us
Back to Heaven and thee.

This epitaph was sent in by Eileen Kemp. It appears on her sister's grave. Katherine died aged 3½.

SLEEP

Let sleep close your eyes till the new morn awakens,
surrender all thoughts and the cares of today.
Forget all the heartaches that clouded your daydreams,
let the soft wings of peace waft your troubles away.

Dream perfect dreams of all that you yearn for;
climb, magical, mystical, paths to the moon.
Drift slowly away to an island of pleasure,
or the sun-kissed sand of a purple lagoon.
Circle the stars on a rainbow of colour,
then flutter away on a butterfly's wings,
or walk leafy lanes hand-in-hand with a lover,
to a crock full of gold while a nightingale sings.

Sleep, perfect sleep, will soften the sorrow,
for loved ones you've lost guard each step of the way,
and its only in dreams can you hold them and keep
them,
till the angels of dawn steal them softly away.

Denis R. Muir

2 October 1988

'only time will heal and so will sleep..'

AFTER A MISCARRIAGE

No name, no face, no date of birth,
No hour of death, no plot of earth.
You never breathed or kicked or cried
And yet for us, you lived and died.
I have a small remembrance
A clinic card, filled in just once.

Fiona Marsden

MADONNA AND CHILD

I
are one in a womb of stone-
bianca del mare - whiteness of water
and stone in which love is.

Faces and hands hold, touch
in total tenderness.
Sheltering arms

offer brief safety.
Her eyes and delicate mouth
prepare for grief.

II
I do not know their dolour -
mothers who live on
when their grown child is dead.

But when a baby died,
fell lifeless from me
before he saw the world

beautiful and cruel,
my grieving arms
felt emptied of flesh.

Anne Born

The Madonna and Child sculpture at St Ives' church, Cornwall, was carved in memory of Barbara Hepworth's eldest son Paul, killed in an accident while flying for the RAF in Thailand in 1953.

ECLIPSED BY EARTH

The sun seemed quite superfluous,
the horned moon's perfection gone
- from your eyes a deeper light now shone;
when you were global - round.

The morning bucket, cravings in the night,
those soft, cupable, breasts turned hard as melons
quite grotesque. We smiled at some of this
but not for long...

Perhaps your body, deep, reviled this passenger, bound
umbilical till -
five billion cells then sought the light
    and after twenty hours of sweat and pain
    slipped only - global -
    back into the ground.

Dave Garbutt

11.4.90

IN MEMORY 5

Though you never lived to see the shifting sunlight, hear
the whistling winds or feel sand beneath your bare feet,
Though no stone marks your passage through life,
Though your ashes have not mingled with the damp
earth from which you sprang,
Though nobody knows your name but us ,
We love you, we know you well, you are our children.

Though your father never read you bedside stories,
Though I never sang you lullabies,
Though we never saw you go to school, nor watched
you run on Sportsday,
Though we never heard you laugh, nor saw you cry,
In the vastness of forever, you have been and always
will be our children, and one day, we will meet you face
to face.

Andrea McAlister

25 October 1990

Written in memory of two babies who were lost through miscarriage within 6 months of each other.

FOR ANGIE, WHO'S BABY LIVED BEFORE BIRTH

Emma has died.
Died before birth.

Sounds she heard;
 A voice tapping on rib pipes,
 in slow, soft notes.
 A breathing, a change of pace.
 The body preparing
 for birth.

She answered;
 letting her thumb
 finger tongue.
 She spoke in small tremors.

She was safe in middle earth,
Her burrow smoothed edged,
Feet and hands spun her around its walls.
She would have known dizziness.
Smiled at movement,
frowned if sound from
beyond her boundaries
vibrated her burrow.

Emma has died.
The nursery is empty.
Tears flow; projected images
lie on cot, inhabit shadows.

Somewhere at the hospital
a filing cabinet
holds her details.
Emma, it says
Born Dead.

A tracing of her activity
should have been taken.
'Lived before Birth'
would have been better
to bear, than the certificate
of death..

Pauline Hawkesworth

MISCARRIAGE: FIVE MONTHS

Two weeks ago your womb pushed up
like a burial mound
even your smock with its autumn russet
smelt of earth.

I remember Avebury
and that long ago plundered tomb
where I lay between stones like ribs
fitting flesh to earth
beckoning back each scattered vertebra.

If I could
I would take apart these days
wheel stones like stars, backwards,
leave you with more than the wind
rushing.

Jenny Vulgar

OLIVE

I didn't cry the moment you were born,
But sometimes now,
Looking down
As you suck or yawn,
My tears come in for you,
Olive, our little third-time-lucky.

Would we love you quite like this
If you'd come easy?
Did we need the sadness to know the bliss?
To think - a short bit
Of nylon tape
Kept you sewn in for us!

You will stay, won't you,
Funny fresh warm puffball,
Precious Miss Worth-waiting-for,
Olive,
Our little third-time-lucky.

Ros Kane

1986

WESTMINSTER HOSPITAL

The suburbs have not pity;
in Twickenham every street held pyres.
I've walked between them often,
other years,
and not been perturbed.
Seen nothing in the year's buds
cut still tight
to see.
Just thought it right
to prune back hard
and make a better show.

This year the first damp smouldering
caught me.

They die so hard
in this ward.
Running away from death
with tottering gait.
They've tried all
and nothings left now
but the winter wait.
When the last frost is past
they'll lay them out.

Some buds never bloom
but must be cut out at the heart.

Jenny Vulgar

GOODBYE SPIRIT BABY

Goodbye child. Goodbye spirit baby.
Your mother does not like to terminate
your life at this early stage, but her life
is more developed, more formed, than yours.

You can go back to being part of love,
after all, that's how you came.
Your only mistake was in choosing the wrong time.
You won't be damned for that.

You are an orange nasturtium, glistening fish,
tadpole, song. I will have you again
another day, when I have time to love you
and a father to give you.

A womb is not enough protection my lovely.
You must go back to the Father,
he was not looking when he sent you. Return,
another time, when I am wiser to be your mother.

Amanda Eason

GOD SPEED OUR JUDGEMENT DAY

Our little baby left us
Before we had a chance to meet,
We didn't even cuddle him
Our little one so sweet.
God called him back to heaven
Before he was ever born,
But we'll recall his birthday,
And evermore shall mourn.
The brothers and the sisters
You never got to see
They miss you baby, just because
You're not at home with me.
Your grannies and your Granddads
They shed their tears for you.
If only my little darling
You could have made it through.
But God saw fit to take you,
And who are we to say
That we'll never meet again
God speed our judgement day.

Carol Watton

Written when Carol's sister lost a child through miscarriage.

FOR HARRIET

I'll never hear our daughter cry
or see a tear fall from her eye,

I'll never see that first short step
or feel her nappies soaking wet,

I'll never hear her call out dad
if in the night her dreams are bad,

I'll never ever hear her chuckle
or watch her hide when she's caused trouble,

To never show her a country lane
or cuddle her warm if soaked by rain,

No sand castles will I build with her
or christmas pudding help her stir,

Now I'll never be filled with pride
if she became a blushing bride,

All these thing I'll never have
our daughter's gone and I'm so sad.

Mr Saunders

After 14 years of infertility Harriet was a dream come true, but it was not to be, she lived for just 3 days.

OUR CONNECTION WAS SEVERED 14

Our acquaintance
was unlucky from the start;
in the very first week
I was sick as a dog for you,
grumping away in my stomach -
insatiably.

By the third month
the strain began to tell;
like an alien invader
you drained my resources,
my inadequate resources.
By the fourth month
it had all gone wrong.
The doctor said: "Your health is in danger;
the baby will be abnormal
(in the unlikely event it survives).
My advice is, Mrs Smith,
we should terminate now."
So she-he-it was terminated.
Our connection was severed.

You came at the wrong time,
to the wrong person.
It wasn't really **my** doing,
that you were misdirected.
I posted you 'return to sender'...
may the universal powers
take you to their hearts.
And may your light spark of life

be blown to flame again,
in a luckier time.

For that short while
you were flesh of my flesh...
Sometimes I see
a small, squashed face
pressed against the glass
of the lighted shop window of life.
Then the bitter tears stream down
like broken waters.
The waters break, bitter and resurgent...
Had you lived,
you would have wept harder, wept longer.
My eyes shed your tears,
my body bears your pain.

It is all I can do.

Fay Chivers

Previously published in 'No Holds Barred', the Women's Press 1985.

THE LOST CHILD

a woman, wild-eyed, wandered
wondering
why the child
the child of truth in her arms
had died

she had felt so sure
so elated
in her labour
and then her breasts were dry
she did not nurture the child
and the truth lay sleeping

the woman
hair neglected, eyes wild
the woman cried

until she heard a voice
saying
share
give the truth away

but it was mine the baby was mine
she said

an animal lay forgotten in the compound
alone
whimpering, starving, unloved
in utter loneliness

the woman
insane with her anguish
thought she would die

she lay down
but she could not rest
she paced and called
and mumbled
and screamed

until
    until
until finally she let go

and another child and another truth was born.

Angie Power

Written after a miscarriage in 1983.

HAIR SO DARK AND CURLY

18

Hair so dark and curly
Such perfect little feet
As beautiful a baby
I have yet to meet.

Fingers long and slender
A little button nose
So complete and wonderful
Including tiny toes.

The memories so precious
Of hours spent with you
A gorgeous little baby
That no one really knew.

Sue James

In loving memory of Darren David James stillborn 14 June 1987.

FULL OF FLOWERS

The day you first entered this cruel world of ours
It felt like our garden was all full of flowers
The sun it shone brightly so high in the sky
And my heart was so happy I thought I would fly
But soon the cruel winter destroyed all our flowers
and where there was sunshine only showers
But though your life ended before it begun
We'll never forget you our dear little son.

Martin Jasiczak

Martin's son was born with heart and brain defects and lived for 9 weeks.

EACH DAY

Each day a little more of you is gone,
Soft clothes would have kept you warm.
I've folded them for you
Kept them away from eyes.
Toys with eyes of glass
Empty smiles would have cheered you,
Turn their faces away,
Names you never had
Have been filed away in the draws of minds,
Never to be spoken,
There was a soft bed
A basket with handles,
It has been put where
It cannot be seen,
A little space for you to lie,
Has been hidden from my sight,
I could not hold you,
I could not touch your skin,
Or hear your voice.
I never even held you,
I hardly even believe in you
Sometimes so empty is the house,
Where we sought to welcome you,
I never had a picture,

You never had a name,
Somehow you never existed
In others eyes,
I could not say goodbye,
Inside there is an empty ache,
Sometimes I feel as if my heart might break.

Juliette

Juliette lost her baby at 28 weeks pregnant.

THRENODY

Though I named you I never knew you
Paul Jonathon (our only son)
my small configuration of heroes.

Like the Witch of Endor I call up ghosts
and tune into frequencies that speak for me:

see you sitting on a bleak stone
chin in hand, awaiting me -
your shade wandering a strange garden
lost in the dark, seeking me.

Poor Jonathon - sucking at honeycomb
flexing muscles optimistically -
stealing a march on sleeping hearts,
the cut and thrust of expectation.

Slipping your shard, you reassessed priorities
heading straight for the mountain-top:
turned your face from our hearth-bound god
and blind light of loving.

Left behind we bob in your wake
as you haul away across the blue -
trawling us quietly after you.

Alison Guinane

I LOVE HER ANYWAY

My Mummy's gone to fetch a sister
(She must like me alot! -
She sent a present yesterday
Some building shapes with slots).

Today my Daddy came and said
She's been delayed on route
She cannot come herself, but hopes
To send a substitute.

I'm sure I'll love the one who's sent
I loved her anyway
And in the end I know that I
Will play with her someday.

Malcom Aveyard

Written when Rachel's sister was stillborn on 13 March 1969.

EMPTY ARMS

I knew you were there from the first:
A tiny seed, sown in love
Growing in the warmth of my womb.

I felt your first hiccup of life
And watched you exercise against my body.
I talked to you during the long days
And cradled you in my bed at night.

And we grew together, you and I,
In those precious months we shared.

Problems, they said.
Then pain and panic and more pain
And scurrying feet and hurrying hands.
And suddenly you were gone.

Stillbirth, they said,
And took you away
Before I could touch you, hold you, smell you,
Look upon your little face.

And I was left with a desolation
That could not be comforted.
But worse, so much worse,
With empty arms.

Enid Middleton

Enid's daughter was stillborn over 20 years ago.

THE TEARS, PUBLIC

You were between a seed and a being
and since you were an unperson
we condemned you to earth with maimed rites
and dispensed with the ordinance.

But the emptiness of your departure
is as great as if the heavens
had been halloed with chants and cries
and the tears we shed were public.

Paul Berry

KAREN

It was the time of roses
When Karen's bright bud
Scattered its petals
Among the flowers of her youth,
Her gaiety, her summer laughter.
We must remember the way
The hedgerows bloomed with wild rose,
Briony, pale foams of meadowsweet,
On the day when she reached
The cool paths of a distant garden.
Let us imagine her brightness
Caught in the glittering shimmer
Of sunlit leaves,
As she moves,
Her young grace unmarred,
Into the rose-light of her new morning.

Joan B Howes

Written when Joan's neighbours lost their young daughter in a road accident.

LOST GRANDCHILD

A breath of sorrow
on the heathered wind
catches my breath
and turns a picnic Sunday
into dust.
That lost child cries
who never breathed
our air
and evening sundown
holds my own child's grief.

Who can I pray to now
for help?
Nature is merciless
and cruel.
While others kneel in church
I call to her
from these familiar hills
but as the dying sun
goes down
blackening the trees
against a saffron sky
I hear no answer.

Deirdre Armes Smith

PREMATURE ARRIVAL

What strange coming was this,
Swelling up like a huge balloon,
Barely able to see over my belly in the bath.
The visit to the Doctor, feeling like a fraud
And later, in the hospital, laid up,
realised your vulnerability and cried.
A false alarm maybe and then whoosh...
a flooding.
"Any pain killers? Pethidine?"
All too late, and
your arrival heralded not by cries
but a blue tube and a hermit's home - a medical
invasion.
Life without mum in the mum machine,
till parents without child in grief valley.

Paula Cruttenden Haines

November 1990.

ANGELS OF THE HEART

(Eleanor's poem)

I refer to her as an angel;
to keep madness from the door.
A golden transmogrification
and a dead child
in sublime glory
grows up and out of our sight,
eternally blessed.

We cannot know
where tender spirits
find their rest.
They are best left in celestial places.
And we look ever heavenward
transmitting our unrequited love,
searching the sky for a sign
to hang our prayers upon.

But when the sky is black
and Heaven seems out of reach
We call our angels home
to the most accessible spot
to live in our hearts forever.
Angels of the Heart.

Lesley Harris

FRIDAY

The tears are there,
I hold them in.
Fridays back to haunt again,
That fatal night my boys were born
Fear, fright, desolation all were here,
The night my boys would appear
Ripped apart within my womb,
Joel first to die so soon,
They fought in vain to make him breath,
His mothers touch he did not feel.
Next came Callum small and red
Mouth open wide to yell his head,
I touched, I felt my son was mine.
Stitched and wheeled within that room
And in my arms my dead son ruled
A cry escaped between my lips
A banshee wail,
All this time for this.
I clutched him tight against my breast
My son, my boy
Don't leave, don't rest.
His tiny hand engulfed in mine.
We'd be like this to the end of time,
A trickle of blood ran from his mouth
Breath again, breath I'd shout
But in my heart I knew the score
My baby son was here no more.
Softly kissed upon the brow,
He'd never feel it, no not now.

His little heart would not keep going on,
So Joel Adam was dead and gone.
On Friday he'll be one that day
With brother Callum to share the day
I can't pretend that I won't cry,
For the one that lives, and the one that died,
But I must remember on that day
Two little candles for each birthday.

Sue Fishpool

Sue's twins, Joel Adam 5lb 10oz and Callum Joseph 3lb 2oz, were born 7 weeks premature.

MELANIE AND MICHELLE (AUGUST 1979)

Infinite beauty in two babies, so small;
Breath-taking wonder that they sleep there at all.
Through misty-wet eyes and the pains of the birth,
I gaze at my daughters - two angels on earth.
Tiny heads cradled in dark curly hair,
Rosebud mouths open, gulping down air.
With skin oh so perfect - so pink and so smooth,
And fragile limbs stretching, learning to move;
Eyes tightly shut, they concentrate deeply,
'Life's such hard work,' they seem to sigh sleepily,
Little chests heaving, struggling for breath,
Tiny lungs fighting for life to cheat death.

How can two children, so pretty, so sweet,
With minuscule toe-nails adorning their feet,
And palms etched with lines for the whole world to see,
Have battled their way from my womb out of me?
Inside they were safe and secure and alive,
Now it's up to them, how can they survive?
I prayed to the God who had sent them to me,
That they should have life and eternity,
If love can move mountains, they surely will live.
My heart throbbed with all of the love I could give.
If I could just touch them and give them my kiss,
So their mother's deep love they could experience - not miss.

But my heart was frozen - it was not meant to be,
For Jesus said: "Suffer the children to come unto me."
And He took them both then, to a new life above;
And all I had left of them, was a heart full of love.

Janette Hill

Michelle lived for 2 days and Melanie for 11 days.

COT DEATH

Today my darling you slept late
the birds sang,
your sister chattered while
you stayed still.
I kissed your cheek, snowflake soft and cold.
Life moved on
you stayed an island of peace, withdrawn,
here yet gone.

Had I not slept
would you be with me still?
Could I have held you to life
as once I held you in my womb?
How could the struggle for birth and joy of life
end in this calm submission
this quiet acceptance
of death?

I live, you die
Will time heal?
Each year another might have been
to mourn again.
Not for us life's frosty separations,
generation wide ideologies,
school days, drugs and motor-cycle fears,
you will grow older only in my heart.

Mine for ever,
loved, cherished, caressed,
nurtured tenderly,
held secretly,
growing perfectly.
Only an empty shell
slowly decays
in sandy Suffolk soil.

Roberta McAuley

ON THE LOSS OF NEWBORN TWINS

A little bit of Heaven came your way,
But unfortunately, not to stay.
Two little angels with damaged wings,
Flew into your heart, pulling its strings.

Two little strangers from paradise,
Had lost their way, and thought 'twould be nice
To visit you, till their earth time was spent,
Alas from Heaven they were only lent.

Now in Jesus arms, they are safely back,
Nothing in earth or Heaven will they lack.
He'll guard and cherish them every day,
And with the cherubs they'll always play.

These two strangers you'll never forget,
Though such a short time with them, you met.
A place in your heart will always be there,
And you will remember them in prayer.

Now at this time of your deepest need,
Stay close to the Lord, for He will heed.
The veil will be lifted, your tears be dried,
He's close beside you, right at your side.

Reach out, touch Him, hold on to His hand,
You may think others don't understand.
Its just that they don't know what to say,
But their thoughts are with you, day by day.
But, in God's own good time perhaps
Another angel will fall in your laps.
One that is strong and able to stay,
Giving you many a laugh each day.

Mrs E Squire

IN REMEMBRANCE

I picture you as a baby
in an incubator connected to
life -supporting wires and
wonder how much damage
excess fluids did to your brain.

Could we have fallen out over
sisterly arguments, swapped
clothes or make-up, shared jokes?
Or would you have been
a source of ridicule?

As each anniversary passes
I comfort myself with
the knowledge it was
kinder that your first
hours were also your last.

Emma Barford

GOODBYE MY SON

As I sit here with broken heart
I wonder how our God could part
A mother and her baby son
Whose partnership had just begun.
You'd learned to smile
And pull my hair
A mother knows how much I cared.
I held you from your birth to end,
My little baby, my little friend.
As daddy said "Goodbye My Son"
I thought we'd never carry on.
We miss you so our little man
And hope we'll join you when we can.
Until that day please do take care,
And know that we are always there,
If you need us we'll be here,
To kiss away your angel tears.
Forever you'll be in our hearts
There's nothing can keep us apart
So baby until we meet again
Our love for you will ease our pain.

Carol Watton

ETERNAL REST

Bleak is the place of eternal rest,
for those on the looking side.
On top of a hill,
breathtaking is the view.
A patchwork of fields, carefully tended.
Meandering paths,
A cathedral in far view,
A scattering of houses,
Rain,
A mule.

The place! The actual God forsaken place!
The horror of seeing
where one's beloved sleeps.
Marked by numbers!!
Anonymous.
Except the earth shattering quake
of the heart
renewed.

Stone upon stone upon stone,
And tombstones? A few.
But for the numbers
to mark the end of a long life
or that , that had hardly begun?

Please care.
Remember her.
My daughter lies there.
In that clean, well tended, sterile land.
Under stone.
Marked by just
A Number.

Mariella Cassar

7.9.86

Mariella lives on the Island of Gozo - Malta. Her daughter was born two months premature and lived for 30 minutes.

TO A.S. for IMOGEN

I came and sat with you and cried,
felt honour in such fellowship,
if honour be the word:
to be allowed to share in pain
that should have been delight,
where, by rights, the only tears
should have sprung from Imogen.
All babies cry.
And we cried, side by side.
I tried to use her name:
I thought it might just help you
in your grief, to hear it spoken.

She was a fighter; lived for several hours.
        Your pride was fierce.
She kicked so hard she should have lived.
        I tried to speak of God
but shared the void where,
in your fear,
your baby floated, motherless,
and blamed you for not being there.
While you, I knew, more needed her
than she now needed you,
yet still I sat with you and cried,
        and had to speak of God.

Celia Warren

For a long while, after I'd buried her,
I didn't like the sound of church bells.
I didn't like the sound of a drum
or the sound of a clock. I didn't like
any sound that sounded endless - as if
it could go on and on and on and on -
and yet, like a child's heart, could stop.

Now, after the years have gone - all three
of them - I can't say I like the sound
of bells, drums or clocks, but I can say
I rarely hear them, except when they stop.

Peter Bradford

Peter's daughter, Tjitske, died age 7.

COFFIN

Your father once built you
a house for your dolls.
But the house was big enough for you.
And so, in your blue bonnet
and your purple blouse
you played in your house,
you laughed in your house,
and some nights, you slept
in your house.
Your house had a window,
a roof, a door and four walls.
You loved your house.

Who built the house
you lie in now?
Sides, walls, roof, floor
but no window and no door -
no way out and no way in.
Who built this house?

Whoever built the house
you lie in now
never knew your play,
your eyes, your laugh.
For if he'd known,
he would have left you
a window,
and a door.

Peter Bradford

TO ELINOR

Had you not died, you would be thirty-three
and, like the rest
now far away from me.
- 'Phone calls, a Christmas visit at the best.

Childhood is a chrysalis that cannot last.
Marked by heredity,
the creature sheds its cast
and when the wings are dry, will flutter free.

Time dulls the edge of loss; though scars remain
these wounds are cold.
Nothing to match the pain
of losing you when you were six weeks old.

That year I haunted paths of loneliness
in a strange city
whose sky was colourless,
tormented by a kind of guilty pity.

We need no graven stone to tell us where
your bones are laid.
We know you are not there ...
But memory grows flowers that will not fade.

Joan Smith

IS IT WELL WITH THE CHILD?

Dear Lord.....it is the child..
I'm writing to you, telling you all my heart -
My poor torn heart, so tempest-tossed and wild,
Left to me desolate.
Faith, sore-eyed and distressed
Forgets her high behest,
Hope, ready to depart,
And only love remains
As warm and wistful now as in the days
When little Dancing Feet slid down the household ways,
For, Lord, You took the child,
I do not reason with you, tho' for that,
But here's my plaint, just this:
I ache for news. There, in the heavenly bliss,
How is it with the child?

Long days I sat
So still, in the still house, and said no word
And if you spoke to me, I never heard
But now, to-night,
I'll sit alone, and let my soul indite
This letter to my God....

I want to know
About the child, - I, Lord, who loved her so.
My spirit always sang
When her dear voice out-rang,
And something in me cried
When small ills came and settled at her side.

I tended her, - yes, hair and hands and toes,
I knew her, sleeping, waking, planned her clothes,
And it is I, Lord, I, who ask some sign,
Some tidings of the child who once was mine,
For I was nearer her than any other -
Her mother.

II **THE REPLY**

Dear Soul....I have so many things to say
But yet you cannot hear them, not today.
I know, and understand
The promise that My hand
Shall help and strengthen seems far off and strange,
At best a poor exchange
For those remembered days,
For all the dear one's wiles and pretty ways.
Yet, let your spirit come
To Me.....to Me,
There is no other in the universe
Who can your comfort be,
For who in all the universe could prove so skilled and fit
To mollify the broken heart as He who fashioned it?
You sat so still, and wondered all the while
How she would fare without your kiss, and smile;
You were so joined to her, you half forgot
That I was there.
I comprehended her when you could not;
I knew her every hair.

Think back. The night before the darling came
You cried to Me. You called upon My name.
That helpless passionate word
I, the Life-giver, heard;
And you, poor wrestler, found your faith prevail,
The Little Ship set sail -
Yes, ventured forth into life's stormy sea,
Bound by the limits of mortality.
Listen poor heart. That far sweet love is past,
I am the First! I also am the Last!
I gave her first faint breath,
And in the love of death
I wrapped her round, and, loving, held her fast.

Down all the ages, not a fledgling bird
Has fallen as it flew,
But I, its Maker, felt My being stirred.
I, the All-Loving, knew
The child- the child, is by Me
Oh, then come
To Me, the only lawful Medium.
She walks the glory-side of Me; so, to the other
Come now; come near, poor broken-hearted mother

News of the child? How is it with her? Where
Is God's high heaven? What is she doing there?
Why if I told you, if I let you see
The radiant joys she has for company;

If I should draw aside
The curtain, leave the casement open wide
For just one moment, flesh and blood would fail
So, in His love, the Father hung the veil
Some blessed day it shall be rent in twain,
And you shall come unto your own again.
'Tis true!. Most true! Oh, let this thought unfold you,
That if it were not so, I would have told you

Then, till that day, that love of joy so sweet,
Can you trust Me with little Dancing Feet?
Behold My hands! Are they trustworthy? Why?
Be not afraid, beloved...it is I.

Eva Torr

Sent in by Geoffrey Rowson. Written by his mother after his sister's death aged 2, in 1936, and discovered after his mothers death in 1976.

IF THE SUN SHOULD BURN
(For Andrew)

If the sun should burn to blackness both my eyes
And the full-phase moon condemn my sight to stone,
Should this winter's wind catch vision by surprise
And the snow fall on these lids, turn them to bone,

All past images of you would congregate
In a heart whose heart has always been in shade,
And a light enormous, then, would emanate
That is love itself, my son, from magic made.

I would learn to braille my way to where you are;
In the peaceful passage of some umbral space,
I would look for love beyond time's farthest star,
And the fingers of my soul would find your face.

As in woodlands there are countless kinds of wings
There are many ways, my dearest child, to see
All the inside-outs, the underneaths of things.
So, then, let those darknesses descend on me.

I will hear the snow and bid the cold adieu;
I will taste the sun and know the sun is you.

Joan Owens

But feel the sweet and tender touch
of a child's kiss.
Offered in innocence.
Softer than silken petals.
Warmer than summer rain.
Cooler than spring showers.
Bestowed with love.
Which heart could withstand
the fond farewell
of one's beloved child.

Ted Harrison

Ted's daughter, Dawn, died age 14 of a brain tumour.

MUM LESS CHILD

Dearest Lord of Heaven, please listen to my plea,
A faithful servant I have been, then why do this to me.
My mind is full of sadness, my heart is full of pain,
I beg you in your mercy, please Lord will you explain.
Why did you take my little girl, my child with eyes of blue,
Did you notice something special, did she steal you heart too
Her charming disposition, her gaiety, her smile,
As all who knew and loved her, did you she too beguile.
The pleasure that she gave me, as she cuddled near,
Did you need a bright new angel, was it easy to choose her.
Her mind so pure and gentle, such pure unselfish love,
Had you searched the whole world over, have you found a pure white dove.
Lord help me in my longing, please help me ease the pain,
I see your need, but Lord indeed, my loss has been your gain.
They say you're kind and gentle, you're love is given free,
I know its true myself Oh Lord, please take this gift from me.

I trust you with my baby, her life I give to you
With her you'll see much clearer the meaning of love true.
Take care of her Oh please my Lord, till we are reconciled,
Please love her fond, please love her long
My own sweet precious child.

Keith Harrison

Written in memory of Gladys who died aged 8 from diphtheria.

WATCHING THEIR LAUGHTER LIVE
(For Easter Barrett and Nicola Goad)

Watching their laughter live where others play
Sharing their game, my contribution small
Learning to give more than my words will say,

Sensing the hurdles of the day to day
I knew how easy it would be to fall
Watching their laughter live where others play.

Beyond the tears, yet only love away
Two faces span the width of times recall
Learning to give more than my words will say.

Such energy that friends cannot betray
A rough and tumble skirmish for the ball
Watching their laughter live where others play.

For them the final game was under way
Before the Friday evening free for all
I learn to give more than my words will say.

Burnishing gold memory from grey
My open hands are breaking down the wall
Watching their laughter live where others play
Learning to give more than my words will say.

John Calvert

She laughed and played, with those we could not see
Her little mind was not as it should be
And in her great simplicity
Knew no real love for me.

Then Jesus learned and took my child from me
Saying I will give her the serenity
And knowledge born to those
Who love with me.

Our darling plays and laughs with those we cannot see
Her little brain is clear, her body free
And she looks down with Him
In grateful love for me.

F E Jordon

This poem was written by Melanie's Granny who dedicated it to her own daughter, Mrs M James, after Melanie died aged 3.

THE EXTRA MILE

You knew I was your teacher
and would come. Together we
would learn to thread a bead,
to use a word again.
So much I had to learn
about a tumour in the brain
and how to use
a word like hope, some more.

The day you cried, "Oh dear,"
knees crumbling to the
crimson, autumn carpet
I saw the anguish in
your mother's eyes
reflect your own six years.
I turned to hide the faith
I prayed to keep.

"He's still my Christopher,"
your mother said.
People stared at your gigantic face
"He's still my Christopher,"
she whispered
to the stars.
"He'll be my Christopher,
even when he's dead".

You painted London buses
and talked of Thomas.
Tank engines filled your head
and made it huge.
I taught you how to hold a brush,
splattered paint upon a page,
to leave your mark.

Each daily task took longer.
One night you couldn't make it through.
You travelled that last mile alone.
You're still our Christopher,
who taught us all we ever need to know.

Wendy French

BY YOUR SMALL COFFIN

By your small coffin,
stony-faced.

The large occasion, the set piece
without power to disturb -
only a public numbness;
but small, unexpected things
catching you off guard -
the wax crayon behind the radiator
(Washable, Non-Toxic' -
what fine vermilion scrawls you gave us!)
the crumpled sock at the back of the drawer -
pin-pricks
like a blade to my heart
that can draw no blood,
but not tears ...

The tears that might relieve
never fall;
perhaps I'm afraid
to drown.

One of my friends survived Auschwitz.
Whoever cried there was finished.
She never cried;
and now she's lost the power to cry.
(She peels onions now and again
to wash away the dust
from the tear ducts).

Tears denied me,
I looked up to the skies;
and, raw, receptive,
saw briefly into the pure distance
where life and death are merged;
and bright among the mingled strands of meaning,
where Belsen buried innocence for ever,
love and death together
shone like flame ...

And when I looked away dazzled
I thought I felt your tug at my coat,
and the tears came.

Fay Chivers

THE QUEST OF ANTHONY DIMITRIUS

He began his pilgrimage in Winter's December
Journeying silently through the dark hours
Over rough terrain.
Steadfastly he continued his even pace
As the weather mellowed for Spring's promise
And Summer's warmth.

As season followed season he progressed slower,
The appointed path arduous and harsh
Virgin, unyielding.
Low hung the clouds, cruel the ground he traversed,
Weakness made the lessening distance
Seem twice as long.

Strength slowly ebbing he travelled into the dark
Unknown cavernous depths, then emerged
In lush pastures.
Beauteous peace, balm for his tired body;
He drank from the fountains, welcoming rest
His quest fulfilled.

His loved ones gathered in a small village church
On a Maundy Thursday for a service
With hymns and prayers.
While words were spoken of courage, love and caring
Misty eyes rested on the small white coffin
Of Anthony age four.

Lily Gardner

Lily is Anthony's grandmother.

ON FINDING AN ANONYMOUS WREATH

Who are you?
Why did you leave a wreath
on our baby's grave?
You are not anyone we know
Did you have so many wreaths
that you spared one for a quiet grave?
or had you a baby that died
and have no grave of your own to visit
so chose ours?
Whoever you are
whatever your reason
we thank you for your kindness
Share not our sorrow
but share our joy
knowing that our baby
is not in barren soil
but in a many-mansioned place
where we through grace may follow on.

Gerald England

Ruth died age 3 weeks. From The Rainbow and Other Poems, Fighting Cock Press, Heckmondwike 1980.

UPON A SMILING DAWN

Can this be right,
this symbolism?
That a suckling infant
should be cut adrift
to glide out helplessly
and alone - clasping Teddy -
on those dark deep rivers?

Crawl bewildered
in his babygro
through vast cathedrals
that gape with ideologies
undreamt of, that echo
with stone-cold indifference
towards an unformed morality?

Float weightlessly,
blink dismayed
at his peers in the void,
awaiting an arbitrary fate?

As a love is laid to rest
let it be just so,
with thumb in mouth,
to dream to all eternity
upon a smiling dawn.

John Arnold

WERE YOU THERE?

Were you there when my little son was born,
When he gave us his very first cry,
The first breath he took and his very first look?
Did you know he was going to die?

Were you there when my little son smiled,
when he held tight around someone's thumb,
as he followed your eyes and gazed in surprise?
Did you know that the end would soon come?

Were you there when my little son spoke,
when he gurgled and cooed in his chair,
when he held up his arms he could offer no harm?
Did you know he was suffering then?

Were you there when my little son cried,
with the constant battering of pain,
when he screamed with alarm as they held out his arm?
Did you know it would all be in vain?

Were you there when my little son died,
when he breathed his last breath on that day?
Did he know who we were or was life just a blur?
Did you know? Was it written that way?

Anne Savan

EPITAPH FOR EMMA

64

Death speaks from the mouths
of robed men.

Oracled in incense
decorous reverent

anthropocentric text
magisterial Latin

and not the tongue of pure
demotic loss, simple unabashed

material response
whispered through bars

at night-time. Not only Emma, born
with half a heart

wouldn't survive the transplant:
her memory pads on iconoclastic paws

digs with small claws
in churchyards.

Alison Guinane

A vicar who banned the words "Goodnight Kitten" from the headstone of a four month old girl was overruled by church authorities after a protest by the child's parents.

IN MEMORY OF ELLEN GAFFNEY

With her came joy and gladness
That cheered our humble home;
Her little baby prattle
Shed light upon our gloom
She tempted us to love her
As if but to decoy
Now death has come and blighted
The object of our joy.
Alas! The joy and gladness
That accompanied her stay
Are replaced by grief and sadness
No solace can allay
A broken hearted father
She left here to condole,
A half-distracted mother
Whom nothing can console
Three loving little brothers
And a sister ever kind
She's gone to join the angels
And left us all behind
She's gone to join the angels
And mingle in the throng
In praise of God and Mary
One voice more in the song.

Written by Ellen's father, in copper plate, when Ellen died, aged 2, on March 12th 1885.

Sent in by H Povall.

High up in the heaven among the stars
There dwells our little Brett
Chosen by God he is to us, the most special angel yet
Like other angels in the heavens he has his tasks to do
Such as colouring a rainbow and sprinkling flowers with dew
Running through the woodlands to make the bluebells ring
And painting robin's redbreast and helping thrush to sing
And on a dark winters night he helps the world to glow
By switching on the stars to shine amidst the icy snow
To us he is so special and its we he holds so dear
Surrounding us with all his love, unseen but yet so near.

Thelma Clout.

Written for Brett's brother and sister by his grandmother.
Brett died in 1984 at the age of 8 months.

DOMINIC

He was small and dainty
With big brown eyes,
And ginger hair on top!
But he had a destiny
None of us could stop
He liked all kinds of music
And lots of things I'd play
To see his little smiling face
And wash his cares away.

He would sit upon the floor
And play with his 'Happy Apple'
And ride upon my back
As though upon a saddle.
And through all these happy days
We knew about his heart
But never in our wildest dreams
Were we set apart.

I hope you are so happy now
And play your games in heaven.
I'll walk along life's lane
And at the end we'll meet again.

Emma Smith (aged 11)

Dominic died aged 13 months of congenital heart disease.

OF A BROTHER DYING IN MY INFANCY

You were the brother whom I never knew
For in your brief day I was still contained
By the solipsist's bubble of my second year.
Only much later did I learn of you
And question fruitlessly how you would have been -
Active or passive? thinker? football fan?
Lover of art? chaser of careless girls?
Would we have grown together or apart?
Would the Celt in your blood or the Saxon dominate?

These things I'll never know and I am free
To posit your future near to my desire -
That we had walked the same way and yet gained
Each from the other's slant of vision more
Than either singly. No, I cannot mourn
One whom I did not know, but I regret
The unshared moments that your death made so.

Frederic Vansen

GOODNIGHT FOR ANGELA

(Song for a dead baby)

Goodnight, for a little space.
We draw the blind, and, keep going,
Leave you in quiet, knowing
Nothing can ever harm you,
Nor the long dark alarm you.
For like a night-light gleaming
Steadfastly through your dreaming
We set our thoughts to keep
The shadows from your sleep.
You're in the fairy place,
With every baby thing,
Safe from earth's wearying.
For Someone watched above you
To comfort you and love you
And keep you, while He could,
In endless babyhood.
You shall have shining Joys
To play with for your toys,
And every hour shall hold
A lovely thing for you,
Because you'll not grow old,
Where fairy tales come true ...

We leave our thoughts to glow
Like lamps near you; and so
On tiptoe come away.
Goodnight, until the day.

Joan Woodcock

"NAY, LASS!"

"Nay, lass, tha shouldn't ha' done it!
        Why tek thi 'ook an' go ter foriegn parts
Wi' out a word, a tear? Whativer 'twas begun it,
        We would 'ave 'elped. We 'aven't filled our 'earts
Wi' luv o' thee, these twenty year an' more,
        Just fer a bit o' fun. For what tha's getten,
T'trouble is, luv, ther's nob'dy found a cure.

"Nay, lass, tha shouldn't ha' done it!
        T'world is a crewl, cowld, an' bitter place
I't'winter wind. But oft-times under t'sun it
        Teks on a better look. If tha could face
Death in that lonely room, why couldn't ta come,
        Wi' all thi troubled thoughts, an' frets, an' pains,
Back 'oam to us 'ere? It's safe an' warm at 'oam."

B P Luxton

Also published in "A Pulse in the Mind", 1979 by B P Luxton.

MY BROTHERS CALL

They were so little when they died;
jaws clamped, eyes frozen-to.
A second's-worth of hostile light,
fire, shrapnel-sharpened knives,
before the world punched them back into oblivion.
My mother had been thrown across a room,
bomb-blast ringing in her ears.
She lasted through the night
but they, poor victims, lost their chance
to fill their lungs with shelter dust.

I've always wondered, had my brothers lived,
would I have been?
Would I have had my high, bright hours,
felt the keenness of the wind,
clung to my father, circled my mother warily,
castigated both when the mood took me?
Or perhaps
I would have been the ghost,
the speculation,
the quiet thought in an empty room
when the fires were low.

And if we had been three,
how would they have been?
Bouncing-on-the-knee brothers,
hale and hearty, strong-as-oak brothers,
pats on the head, helping with the homework,
hoisting-on-shoulders kinds of brothers:

making me laugh, tying my fears
in a coloured handkerchief
knotted for each frailty.

And as I grew, would they have been
Supportive Men,
proud of my womanhood
yet close,
whispering secrets and yelling my joys.
Would we happily have shared
parental shouts and shoves, pinches and slaps,
those strung-up petty torments
meted out so casually.
Would we have kissed for love,
not just to satisfy a code; seen ourselves as
wild companions on a rugged shore,
each fighting for a different moon
while trading winds for stars?

A blood-bone-skin-stone kinship?

I'll never know.
I can't even visit your graves
for you had none. You weren't supposed
to have lived at all;
and now exist only in my thoughts
and my mother's misted eyes.
Spectres from an entrenched tomb,
you've cried out weakly through the years
for recognition and an epitaph;

and though you freeze my listening bones
your death-place needs no signature,
for you are part of me
and my particular piece of bloodied earth.

Brothers,
I address your memory:
and formally name you, James and John,
to mark your loss in proper state
and give your souls authority.
Take this as your memorial song,
a thank-you for my dance with fate,
and let me claim you, proudly, from
the wasteland of the war-dead young.

Tessa Rose

'a belated "Hello" to two unknown brothers who died at birth during the war'.

I WANT

I want to tuck you up in bed and kiss you goodnight,
I want to lay me down to sleep knowing you're alright.
I want to wake in the morning and hear your little voice,
I want to go and pick you up but I have no choice.

I want to sit and cuddle you and stroke your silky hair,
I want to kiss your warm sweet face and feel you oh so near.
I want to hear you giggle the way you used to do,
I want to hold your body close and put my arms round you.

I want to tell you I love you and we will never be apart,
I want to see that smile of yours it would always melt my heart.
I want to smother you with love and kiss your precious head
All these things I want to do but I can't ....because you're dead!

Dany Sherlock

Mummy, I leave you with every ounce of my love,
I give you all my laughter, millions of smiles -
use them often.
I leave you lots of time -
more time to look after yourself -
time to strengthen your heart and mind -
time to cherish Sarah and Daddy
Go into the world knowing that I
am in your heart - share your love,
use your time wisely,
walk tall and be proud -
Love, smile, talk, sing for me.
Live life to the full - for our love will
give you strength -
I will show you the way,
our time together is over
go in peace - knowing I'll love you
Until we met again.

Linda Walker

Andrew was killed by a lorry as he stepped off a school bus. He was 5 years old.

Settling to write. When the 'phone rings I curse.
'Bad news - our little boy - '
In the flat calm of Sunday morning
The bulk of his loss rises sheer as an iceberg.
I claw for purchase, use words like heartbroken,
appalled.
They scale nothing.
'I'm sorry if I've spoilt you day,' he ends.

With a wide smile
She welcomes me into their small flat,
As if to a party. We hug wordlessly.
Among brimming ashtrays, empty whisky bottles,
It happened in church, she says.
After Harvest Thanksgiving, they went to his pram...
I marvel at the faith that primes her smile.

'You never saw John, did you?' His eyes
Are half-lidded with fatigue, booze and grief.
He has melted into a rush of words, laughter, tears.
I am shown the album. His father in miniature.
Couldn't have children they thought , so adopted.
Then wonderfully - a miracle, it must have seemed -
She conceived, only to lose her peeled, blind foetus.
'We'll try again when she's stronger,' he'd said,
unbitter.
And at last she bore the longed-for child. Now this.

She offers me cake, fag dangling.
'I'd given up' - this time the smile is rueful -
'Hadn't smoked for a year.'
'John Patrick,' he recites suddenly,
'July the sixteenth to September the twenty-seventh.
Two months ten days.
That's all there is to say.'

Except -
In church?
At Harvest time?
Sometimes, God, I wonder at your sense of humour.

Brian Levison.

THE BASKET

He was in a deep blue babygro
the third time I saw him,
had filled out into two-month
contentment, was perfectly at home
among the talk and wine glasses
at my book celebration.

A week later when I was told
he had died a hole was punched in me.
I felt nothing at first,
papered the gape by checking
what bandaging there was
for his gashed parents.
But when I lay down in the dark
water rushed up my gully.

It was later that I saw the basket -
not the wicker basket
though that was there too,
its small sides folded into emptiness -
but an interweaving of arms and trunks.
When I came closer
and touched its extraordinary warmth,
I saw it was lined
with the love and grief of each
one of us cradling
Maggie and Colin crying.

Myra Schneider

Previously published in Cathedral of Birds by Myra Schneider, Littlewood/Giant Steps 1988.

JOHNNY

1

Not nine months' fret, nor eight
Laboured hours could dilute
Amazement at your instant
Or purplegrey emergence:
Eyes clenched above beaked nose, the elongated
Skull of some Aztec or Hittite
Warrior - and I cried
Like a worn-out child.

We made it! Our wait
Of six years, the absurd
Humiliation of infertile
Trials: *this jar for the first*
Part of your ejaculate, the
*Rest...*the unexpected mess
Euphemised as miscarriage, all now
Made sense for making you.

My gloating accounts
Of our triumph by phone
Eroded past snags - until pride,
Full, gleaming like a much-thumbed
Chestnut, gave the lie
To that previous earnest
Disclaimer: A birthchild
Is not that important to me.

II

Sun blazed prodigal
That second morning of your life:
Touched stucco up to mintwhite, spattered
Short-sleeved crowds with leafshade, spilled
Across the hospital bed where you dozed,
Half-curled against her heavy breast, minute
In a lime-green vest. I halted, called...
She opened eyes and smiled.

Fatigue was another country; those night-
Time cries, thin sheep-bleats, trespassing
Into arid dreams - What
This time round? Thick-fingered
Brain ticking off the probable. Your first
Enormous sticky shit, as black
And pungent as rich farmland earth.

Weeks on: your naked feet firm-braced
Against my belly, fingers clenched
Round mine; I smiled,
You danced, I sang
And smiled - until one night
You caught my smile and fielded
It to me as shyly, awkwardly
As an eager-fingered toddler with a ball.

One night you died, away from home
Without warning, aged
Seventy-three days. My bland
Phone manner fractured as she broke
The news obliquely. Futile hopes
Racing in a hospital-bound taxi. Hope
Dead on arrival. *Is he? Yes.*
Our grief collided in that corridor.

Solemn, small once more, your three
Year old big sister gave
A nod when asked if she wished
To see you, shook her head
At Do you want to hold him? I
Could have hugged your half-warm
Body for ever - though I begged
For another time and place.

Life never so intense as then
And there, though. The perverse
Kick of retailing bad news
Down the phone: those shuffling treks
To mute hugs on the doorstep; you
Half-buried by comfort grief; your mother
Clutching, chest high, another jar
Of breast milk destined for the sink.

IV

Leaves flaring in the brief

Space before fall. One week
Beyond your death: a picnic
At wood's edge with friends. Bread
Suddenly unchewable - I sensed
You, a twelve-year boy
Calling from the trees; felt life
A bubble, whole and vulnerable...

Something beyond a sick
Abracabastard's joke comprising
A superior coffin white
Polished with double
Mouldings and plinth. Lined inside
Best swansdown. Limousine
Bearers and personal
Supervision.

Now, five months on, most friends omit
Your name in talk, wait awkwardly
For me to resurrect it. I must grope
Towards meaning alone. Above
Minute narcissus trembling
To my electric typewriter, your sole
Smiling photo warms me - I
Return that smile.

Colin Rowbotham

Maggie Hindley and Colin Rowbottom lost their son Johnny in a cot death at the age of ten-and-a-half weeks. Their experiences are told Life Studies One published by Littlewood Press, 1988.

LOVE'S SORROW

All anniversaries fling us back
To memories tenacious hold.
That patchwork postcard suddenly blurred
Into a sea of senseless words -
A mighty roar of negation
Rose like a bore and sent me spilling.

Now one year has passed:
This solemn meeting point of waning sun
On dial, when time misses a beat
Before inexorably moving on
I come to a new realisation -
Although I never met you
I get a sense of who you are.

Your passage on earth was so fast
You little rocket man
That I begin to think
(For seventy-three days is an age hopelessly out of sync)
That you are some harbinger
Or rare comet - Halley's kith
Locked in a brief earthly cycle
Unkind to kin.

But as echoes announce both parting and arriving
And absence recalls more keenly your presence
Than whenever you were there -
Let the wheel turn
Who knows when you will come this way again?

Susan Mitchell

September 1987

A CANDLE FOR JOHNNY

In the coffee dregs
Like little fingers reaching out for the brim
I saw candles - a cluster of tiny candles.

Outside in the November light
A pink horizontal band curved around the sky
And Montparnasse tower loomed like a pale spectre.

In the dim dome
Dotted here and there
Were patches of light,
Right at the back, discreetly lit
Stood Saint Joseph and his child
And behind, the three stained-glass windows;
Faith, love and advise to flight -
Take Mary and your infant to Egypt.

I added a small candle
A small finger of light reaching upwards
A small thought for a small child
Too soon departed.
But the finger of light held good
And glowed between faith and love
The lights of the city glowed down below

In the dregs of coffee I see candles.

Susan Mitchell

1986

YOU WEREN'T THERE

I drove passed your school
But you weren't there
I saw all your friends
But you weren't there
I came home from work
But you weren't there
I went into your bedroom
But you weren't there
I called out your name
But you weren't there
I feel so alone.

Christine Kenyon

Christine's only son, Jamie, drowned in August 1989 while on holiday with his father and stepmother in Spain.

FOR MY TWIN GRANDCHILDREN BECKIE AND EMMA

The morning that you died,
before even I knew
you sent a message on my window sill

A very small but perfect butterfly
which opened up its wings
our favourite peacock hue.

Was it you?

so many signs of spiritual presence
you have sent to me in the last weeks

in poetry you have written

tucked away in private drawers;
comforting, sustaining and reminding me
we shared so many joys:

childish drawings in old story books
ringed in kisses and loving scribble
"This is Nanna. I love her".

Flowers you picked for me last summer
waiting for me in my old flower press,
pansies for hearts-ease and forget-me-nots.

White flowers that bloomed on the Azalea
that hadn't blossomed for many years -
two perfect virgin flowers:

Two white hyacinths you gave me
Mothering Sunday many moons ago
came among the weeds to cheer me.

But above all the warmth of love,
the great love we had for one another
surrounds me every moment of the day

and I can say without a trace of doubt
that you are with the God that you both loved
and all is well with you.

Barbara Steele

Emma and Beckie died together tragically in a barn fire in January 1991, aged 17.

I MISS YOU SO

I miss you so, my lovely child,
No-one knows how much...
Only when I'm alone
Dare I let my thoughts seek you out
And then it always ends in tears,
Hot tears that make me ugly -
Would make you sad.

I try to hide my grief, for who can help?
Tearful, I am an embarrassment
To those around me, whose halting tongues
Can only murmur platitudes
That serve to indicate deeper feelings
We find hard to express.

Such flippant things surprise me
With a sudden glimpse of you -
A white-socked schoolgirl,
A old pop record or your favourite book;
The skinny child who laughs and leaps,
The pale child in her wheelchair.

So clearly can I see your slender hands,
Slim fingers caressing your beloved cat,
Or busy at the typewriter
Deftly imprinting the flimsy paper
With the substance of your thoughts
And all the bright imaginings of an active mind
Imprisoned in a weakening body.

Why am I not allowed to think of you
Without pain, regret or guilt?
Why may I not remember the happy times,
Unspoilt by the knowledge of anguish?
Why do I need to probe the wound,
Constantly turning the knife point of recollection
In the scarred tissue of my memory,
Testing the hurt to see if pain has lessened?
It has not.

My best was far from good enough,
I always knew it.
But I loved you - do love you -
With my whole being.
"Whole being" - that's no longer true.
The phrase touches the very essence of my state.
I am not a whole being any more.
Without you I can never be complete.

Marianne Privette

Marianne's daughter died aged 14 after a long illness.

The loss of a young son, the heaviest of burdens.
A load to be carried where nones gone before.
The weight of that loss, the heartache and emptiness;
the emptiness mostly that sweats from each pore.
    For gone are the days of watching and holding;
    gone are the weeks of loving and care.
    Gone are the months of growing and stretching;
    lost are the years in an instant somewhere.
    Somewhere away from the reach of our arms,
    somewhere where no-one would dare - only he,
    surrounded by strangers, and why on a carriage
    way?
    Why was he taken? It should have been me.
For he would have carried the loss so much easily,
He would have understood better than I.
He would have shrugged once or twice to his inner self,
and he had the youth and the strength to get by.
    But gone is my son, for ever and ever.
    Gone are the chuckles, the cheek and the grin.
    Silent the footsteps, the scuffing of "wellies",
    the thump at the door before he came in.
    And gone is his bed with two big soft pillows;
    his toys stored away out of sight in a drawer;
    no fire in his bedroom, no portable "tele"
    with him lying fully outstretched on the floor.
Gone in an instant all hopes of tomorrow,
gone are the things he promised from birth.
Lost is the pride in his size and his stature,
gone in an instant to a hole in the earth.

Six foot of soil hides the millions of heartaches,
the stone hides the story of father and son,
and lost is the surname, lost here forever,
inscribed in gold lettering, but hopelessly gone.
All I have here are thousands of memories,
the unbearable pain which I've had from the start,
for here lies my love and my hopes and my Robert;
here lies my Robert - and here lies my heart.

Denis R. Muir

Denis lost his son, Robert, at the age of 15, when he was killed instantly while crossing the road.

TO A DAUGHTER ON HER 13TH BIRTHDAY

May was there a damp affair
between contractions I could hear the plumbers
tramping up and down the hall
unblocking drains, sweeping sewage
off the back lawn.
Afterwards the veranda
flapped with nappies all winter.

Before that I remember
watching rain sweep up the bay
you rippling my skin like wind on water.

At your birth I was delivered,
made over, given a new name.
For weeks I woke on sheets
that clung to my breasts
wet as a baptism.

May on this side of the world
is still moist
but winter is behind us.

Paper table cloths swing like Jacob's
cloak against the long grass. The fatted
calf has turned bright with cake.

Candles are burning but this year
more than other years, I celebrate you here
and not, as I thought in March
when your heart jackhammered your chest,
dead.

That bereavement has no word;
not widow, relict, just un mothered.
From this wet May to something
arid; sand, dust, a dry wind
and the day roofless.

Jenny Vulgar

CHARLOTTE

Good view from this cross-beam-
can see that dreary box they're watching.
Dangle my legs, laugh at the seriousness.

> We sat silent, diverting tearful thoughts,
> read the detailed, loving service sheet,
> eyes drawn hypnotically to the pony
> in white flowers -

Yep, like that, could ride now through early
blue-bells, jump my way to stardom; make
faces at this unhappy lot, make them smile..

> Life was cruel, short, joy and
> innocence swept away in screeched brakes
> and weighted thud on red grass.

There's Mum, Dad, Granny, Becky's Mum shaking,
white damp squares wrung in sadness, thinking
of me....

> Watching others in a misty emotional
> vision, the sprite-like words of Lord
> of the Dance lost in their poignancy,
> crimmond plaintive in its pastural beauty.

Great. Mega. Best hymns and my clarinet that
squeaks in practise, but why don't they feel
my happiness, my lightness - leaving all the
earthly pain and worry?

Strained listening, achievements in so
short a bubbling life, her funny verse
catching at our throats - until her father's
poem spills rain.

Time to go, these curtains tickle. I can jump
groundwards or fly and I'll dance while they
grow old and grey. Why do they cry when their
lives could be filled with love?

We felt her spirit - somewhere close, her
liveliness trying to touch us with some
message, but we couldn't hear her words.

Fay Green

Written on the death of a friends 10 year old daughter.

The Chapel of Unrest

Embalmers have developed quite an art,
an expertise-no doubt to calm one's fears-
so subtle that one cannot tell apart
the living from the dead. For it appears
they've read the deep conviction that one feels
that death cannot be permanent, that one
will find, and soon recover, warm and real,
the infant one has lost, the missing son
just absent at the dawn. So when one comes
and enters to identify one's child
the shock is like fulfilment. One becomes
alive again and radiant, almost wild
with joy and expectation, till an arm
descends upon one's shoulder, with its qualm.

At the Registrar's

The ice itself has turned to a defence
along these streets. The rough suds of the snow
are frozen in the gutter, an offence
to a red eye. I feel I'm split in two.
My head observes the progress of my feet.
In-between is nothing, just a gap
that's open to the wind. I leave the street
and climb up to an office, quietly tap
the hazed glass of a door. An object

has been lost. Its body, though, must go down in
the records. I state its date of birth, eject
the same date of its death. Then stammer, grin.
But why today? It happened, I am sure,
some twenty years ago, or even more.

The Witness Box

High iron rails surround the witness box,
still pen me in. I stand apart, remote.
No doubt it's quite a normal paradox
that innocence feels guilt. And now my throat
has hoarsened. Like a common murderer
I mutter out the details with a choice
of half-objective words, as, through a blur,
the questions come. I hear my low slow voice
narrating how a child lay on its back,
eyes closed, the skin blue-grey, a stain of blood
descending from one nostril as a black
sun rose. Then cough. The words have stuck like mud.
One hundred yards away, behind the door,
grey waves are slowly beating on the shore.

Lectisternium

And now you've placed the toys upon the bed,
a bear with eaten ears, some rattles, rings,
a sort of lectisternium that is spread
through the cold room. It helps one's sufferings.
Things mustn't be suppressed, although a shroud

is smothering our hearts. Inside the wood,
like scraps of fracto-cumulus, old clouds
of snow still haunt the trees. Misunderstood,
I walk as in a dream. Impersonal
I turn my eyes, and look down at the floor.
I seem to see an infant, very small,
that's lying in a distant mortuary drawer.
Its eyes are opened wide. Expressionless,
they stare out at a void of nothingness.

The Comforter

Now February ends. The clouds express
their visible derision and the wind
puts ice into the attic. None the less
I smile and act compassion, state I find
a bliss in death, a blessing. Saying "Yes",
I keep off the commiserating minds
that add their private burden of distress
by way of consolation, in a blind
attempt to shed their terror. Quietly
I sit, continue lying. I invent
strange messages I say I have received,
angelic intuitions. Patiently
I calm the old and grieving. None is sent
away without a comfort, undeceived.

Forgotten Children

Afterwards I thought they were a gift
from God, those intimate forwarnings that
would walk me out at evening through the drift
of rain and take me into graveyard walls
untended and forgotten, the unmarked graves
still showing through the grass. It seemed that all
in time were left abandoned. No one gave
the rotting cross attention, set a cup
to fill with weeds or flowers. There I'd feel
a strange compulsive mourning welling up
like a salt sea: feel disparate, unreal
as a blown ghost. Such things now correlate
with different thoughts. With conscious guilt. With hate.

John Gurney

Previously published in Encounter May 1987

CHRISTMAS IS COMING

Christmas is coming
Just what shall I do?
No plans to make
No toys for you

I dread the thought
Of Christmas Day
Think I'll stay in bed
Till it's gone away

But that's not right
I must see it through
Remembering Christmas past
All shared with you

What fun we had
Each Christmas morn
That day that
Our Dear Lord was born

If I believed in Santa
His reindeers and his sack
I'd write and ask him, please
Won't you bring Jamie back?

Christine Kenyon

DESOLATE

Although the sun may never shine again,
No torrents of interminable rain
Expunge this shock of misery and pain.
Beneath the leaden clouds a frantic cry
Will pierce the solid cruelty of sky
And through the fissure scream an anguished "Why?"
Then struggle through the fragments of belief
To find - there's none, there's never a relief
Or comfort for the agony of grief.
Sweep up life's shattered particles at last,
They will not mould into a time now past;
We are but specks, the Universe is vast
And sad means not more wise, but more perplexed
Yet less prepared for what may happen next.

Imogen Grosberg

Imogen wrote this on hearing that the 3 year old daughter of Gordon Greenidge, the West Indian Test Cricketer, had died.

REQUIEM FOR LOST CHILDHOOD

For all that never was
for rotting leaves and lightening sky
the calm of evening after summer rain
and the pool that will be still again.

For all that could have been
for play and laughter, anger, tears
and paths that cross in shade and
sunlight till the end of time.
For lives that have another rhythm,
another rhyme.

Rain drops into the pool fast and slow
and all I ever know is to let go.

Jennie Milnes

LOSS

Don't offer me
a panacea to pain.
I need to live it
to be free again.

Don't offer me
the Song that
has no ending.
I need to grieve
to go on mending.

Don't offer me
the graveyard
of your heart
to cope with her loss.
I stand on solid ground.
The Cross.

Jennie Milnes

MY BOY SIMON

Simon Adams, what a cheeky lad
Doesn't know his good from bad
Riding bikes and throwing toys
As well as making lots of noise

"He's a typical boy" friends would say
That was until that fateful day
One Monday morning he took quite ill
From that day on my life stood still

Off to hospital we had to go
Our hearts were heavy and full of woe
Doctors came and tests were done
They all proved normal - except one

Meningitis? what does that mean?
Only on telly these things are seen
He's getting worse - what can we do?
Simon Adam - Southampton for you

Brain scans, blood tests and E.C.G's
He really must have all of these?
The troubles a blood clot on his brain
And obviously he's in much pain

The operation was a great success
To Intensive Care for his brain to rest
In the next few weeks he got on fine
Until his birthday at a quarter to nine

More tests and scans and a main line drip
From this world he began to slip
Epileptica, this time they said
Within four weeks my boy, was dead

No more could be done to save my boy
And now I cuddle his favourite toy
I see his face in his sister Sammie
or as he called her, ahh! my Mammie

I miss him so, cry many tears
and suppose I will for years and years
What reason? Why? What did I do?
for my boy Simon was only two.

Sally Crick

IN MEMORY OF DUNCAN
(DIED MAY 1985 AGED 13)

What pointless words could fill the grievous space
(Though May flowers bloom in tangled dewy skein)
Which, in his life, was Duncan's destined place
(Soft lilac perfume scents each English lane).
His summer promise crumpled into dust,
(While blossom dances on the heavy air)
His youthful body left and empty husk,
(As clouds their wash of gentle rain prepare).
But if the storm of pain sweeps all aside
(The ghost of roses fall in fragrant showers)
Then perish all whoever lived and died
(Pellucid Earth brings calm to later hours).
So, rainbow clear his shining days suspend,
Brightness his life, in mystery his end.

Daphne Schiller

TO A SON WHO COMMITTED SUICIDE

He danced with us
for seventeen years -
a flame intense
and flickering - a
point of family pentagon.
The world's winds
blew him both
too high and then
too low, and suddenly
the low became
the loss.

And now is memory
of a gracious
boy - dreams that
see him dancing
through a door -
and grief - our pentagon
now incomplete.

He was so nice, yet
now he will not burn again.
His flame is gone,
His dance is ended.

Andrea Shaw

GRAVE VISITING

Someone before me
lay their bluebells
on your grave.

Did I hear footsteps
skipping past me
as I walked?

I don't believe
you lie beneath
this earth

but that you pass here
sometimes
catching my thoughts.

Frances Nagle

SLEEP

Sleep on
sleep on
sweet Eleanor
and when your
sleep is done

Mummy and Daddy
will be there
with you
and life will have
then begun

For all must sleep
and all must wait
yet time is very fleeting
so sleep on
sleep on
sweet Eleanor
Until we all are meeting

Love Nanny

Xmas 1990

WEEP NOT

Weep not for me,
I am not here
Beneath this stone
You plant for me.
I am above
In sun and shower
I fall upon each
Beautiful flower
I am the warm breeze
on your cheek
I am the happiness
You seek.
Weep not for me
Mother of mine
I am always here,
Just locked in time.

Ann Upex

TODAY IN MY GARDEN

Today in my garden
I planted a tree.
A tree of heaven
That's what it will be.
Each day I shall watch it.
Grow tall and strong.
Each day I shall ask myself.
What went wrong?
My tree of Heaven
Will see me through
My tree of heaven
Was planted for you!

Alison Proctor

April 1986

Alison lost a daughter at 26 weeks pregnant and twins at 19 weeks pregnant.

PURE THANKFULNESS

Break not your heart, for he has not gone,
he's waiting for you when you go.
Shed not one tear for the first stems a flood
that will weaken your faith if it flows.

Search not for sight - for he can't be seen,
but his presence is with you the same.
Call not for him on the darkest of nights,
he would rather you whispered his name.

Heed not the emptiness deep in your soul,
or the numbness of aching despair.
Banish your grief, and the loss - and the pain,
and the helplessness fraught everywhere.

The edges will soften, though never close o'er,
I promise this promise because,
"SAY NOT IN GRIEF THAT HE IS NO MORE,
BUT IN PURE THANKFULNESS THAT HE WAS".

Denis R. Muir,

15/18 March 1990

MY SISTER'S FUNERAL DAY

Reverend Mother asked for prayers
In the Assembly hall where
Tickets were given for good behaviour:
'Excellent', silver-green, 'Good', blue.
Everyone was kind.

I remember the dettol smell,
The empty wicker cradle
In my mother's room,
The coffin white as a christening shawl,
Shaped for a three weeks' length

I remember the jigsaw
They bought me afterwards,
Cottages in snow, candlelit windows.
I clutched it like a prayerbook
On top of the homeward bus from Piccadilly.

Later I would piece the snowscene,
Its tall trees black as certainties.
It remained a puzzle.

A. C Clarke

WHEN ALL THE WORLD 116

When all the world is dark and no light gleams
And all you see is tears - or so it seems -
Hold on - the Spring will come.

When life seems so unfair it can't be borne
And dark is very dark - no sign of dawn
Be brave - the Spring will come.

For suddenly you'll see a mist of green
Upon the trees, where spiky twigs have been.
Blue washed sky - fresh laundered fluffy clouds
Bluebells, primroses and daffodils in crowds.
Its here - the Spring has come.

So when you think the sun will never shine
And things are too unfair for me and mine;
Remember all the love we have to give
Can light up all our dark - long as we live.

Mrs J Freer

In memory of her grandson who died of cot death aged 4 months.

STILL

I still remember
The suddenness of your birth
The sadness of your death
I still see you
In a small and silent world
Struggling for life in a plastic shell
I spoke to you
But you slipped away
Taking bright plans for a future
Leaving a pain that still aches
I still see it
In your Mum, my friend
She still remembers.

Jackie White

7 November 1990

Written the day Jackie came to a babies Remembrance Service at Bath Royal United Hospital.

HEAVEN'S TREASURE

Heaven would not be Heaven
Without the children there
Playing hide and seek in pearly mists
Free of every pain and care.

Heaven would not be Heaven
Without their carefree rapture
Scrambling through the fluffy clouds
Each happy moment to capture.

Heaven would not be Heaven
Without their shouts of laughter
Echoing across Elysium fields
As starbursts they chase after.

Heaven would not be Heaven
Without their joyful choir
Ringing through celestial realms
Sweet voices rising ever higher.

Heaven would not be Heaven
Without their radiant light
Undimmed by earth's murky shades
Their robes are shining-bright.

Heaven would not be Heaven
Without their smiles of pleasure
Bearing sheaves of rainbow flowers,
The children are Heaven's treasure.

Irene Walsh.

Dedicated to Irene's baby who died aged 9 weeks.

BRIGHT STAR

120

I have lost me a jewel from life's diadem,
A wondrous stone-a precious gem,
Formed by the fusion of heaven and earth,
Refined in the fiery pains of birth.

I have lost me a flower from life's bouquet,
A fragrant rose on a sunny day,
Sown by the urge of nature's need,
Heaven's spirit sanctified the human seed.

I have lost me a star from life's evening skies,
So brightly it shone through a mother's eyes,
Yet I know that bright star will blaze a trail,
When I too pass through the darksome vale.

Irene Walsh

Written for a son who died suddenly aged 36.

SILENCE

There is
nothing more
silent
than the moment
following
the final heartbeat
of a child.

Peter Bradford